Minor Loss
of Fidelity

poems by

Peter Caccavari

Finishing Line Press
Georgetown, Kentucky

Minor Loss
of Fidelity

Copyright © 2022 by Peter Caccavari
ISBN 978-1-64662-901-5 First Edition
All rights reserved under International and Pan-American Copyright Conventions. No part of this book may be reproduced in any manner whatsoever without written permission from the publisher, except in the case of brief quotations embodied in critical articles and reviews.

ACKNOWLEDGMENTS

"Viewer Aggression Advised," "This Page Intentionally Left Blank," and "Minor Loss of Fidelity" appeared online at *Cathexis Northwest*.
"Dominion" was a co-winner of the Cincinnati and Hamilton County Library Poetry in the Garden Contest.
"Carole of the Bells" appeared in *The Louisville Review*.
"Gift" appeared on "Conrad's Corner" on WYSO in Yellow Springs, Ohio and WOSU in Columbus, Ohio.
"Come Dew, Come Rust" appeared in *Dappled Things*.

I cannot thank Tyrone Williams enough for his feedback, encouragement, and friendship over the years. This collection would not have happened without him. Thank you for our talks about poetry, which have fed me and made me believe these things could live outside of my head and on the page.

Publisher: Leah Huete de Maines
Editor: Christen Kincaid
Cover Art: Jeff Carson
Author Photo: Jeff Carson
Cover Design: Elizabeth Maines McCleavy

Order online: www.finishinglinepress.com
also available on amazon.com

Author inquiries and mail orders:
Finishing Line Press
PO Box 1626
Georgetown, Kentucky 40324
USA

Table of Contents

Viewer Aggression Advised 1

Corona 3

Dominion 7

Carole of the Bells 8

Jupiter 11

Aubade 12

My New Year's Resolutions 13

Minor Loss of Fidelity 14

The Sky Sheds a Tear Shaped Like a Black Bird 16

Beginning Acoustics 17

Finitude 19

morning, morning 21

This Page Intentionally Left Blank 22

Gift 24

Doing and Undoing 25

Nostalgia and Amnesia 26

Every Road is a Biography 29

My One-Sided Conversation with a Stretch of Limestone
    along I-75 31

Come Dew, Come Rust 33

*For Katie, Grace, and Jack, who are always there for me—
come dew, come rust.*

Viewer Aggression Advised
Castle Hill Avenue, The Bronx, 1989

The day is falling to its knees, hinged against
The pavement whose firmness consoles and bruises.
I roll off the 6 train into the incense

Of spring, walking Castle Hill, which refuses
To be cheered. Two high school girls are up ahead.
Each one in her talk and striding proposes

The canter of certainty to the world, bred
Among the young. I trail the flint of their heels
Which lights my way. Then two cars pass us, noted

When the first brakes at once and the second peels
To the right to avoid the crash but then hits
A stop sign. The first driver seemingly feels

Concern and stops just past the corner. With bits
Of headlight on the ground, the other car's door
Flies open and an arm with a crowbar juts

Out. *Person A travels at the speed of pure*
Vengeance and Person B waits swollen with fright.
Calculate the total joules required to cure

The sum of their amygdalae. Assume flight
Is not an option. Crowbar reaches window
But restrains. Words pass through. They must be the right

Words because, despite what seemed ill-fated, no
Windows or lives are shattered this day. The men
Retreat to their interrupted plans and go

On. Are they changed? Confirmed? Loosened? Stiffened? When
Have we witnessed without missing the crux? I
Think of voice and echo, the same, just cloven

In two by hardened surfaces. The girls cry
Out their judgment. "I don't blame him for being
Pissed off," the one girl says. "Yeah, the other guy

Had it coming," the second girl says. Seeing
No more to comment on, they change the subject.
How solid their fortress, how distant their spring.

Corona

1

When touch became our common enemy
We had forgotten how the world could turn
On us like that, how a candle could burn
As light, then seethe through the house setting free
Its inventive anger, its verity
That will not stop until we come to learn
The truths that we ignore: that love is stern
As death, that death whispers love's calumny.
Even our cataclysms must die one day.
Bubonic plague nearly ran the table
But now is nothing more than a footnote.
We're all in this together, so they say,
For every crisis must have its label,
Although the truth lies deeper in the throat.

2

Although the truth lies deeper in the throat,
The truth will out in water droplets sent
Abroad. Their hang time is parsed, their descent
Measured, their resting state timed as a coat
Forms on surfaces upon which we dote
With disinfectant, ever expectant
Of the next wave. Our fear and ire are pent
Up, our world constricted down to a mote.
So social distancing was our answer
And the question was asked: Who has the right
To call the shots, to tell us what to do?
Libertarians shun any master.
Live free or die, they cry, but soon they might
Find the latter is the one that comes true.

3

Lately what one finds is that what comes true
Is how uncommon the common good is,
How un-past the I-told-you-so past was,
How lifestyle trumps life, how many and few
Tussle in their cage match, a pay-per-view
That keeps the revenue streaming. This pause
Célèbre that refreshes or refracts shows
Us who we are and that not much is new.
There's no surprise that we are a mixed bag
Of flesh, antibodies and pathogens
Vying for their turf, antigens latching
Onto whatever is at hand. The gag
Is we're like that inside and out. To cleanse
Our struggle would be a kind of dying.

4

Our struggle would be a kind of dying
To our former way of living if we
Let it, but do we have the strength to be
That weak? May we never more find boring
Anything or anyone as they bring
Their broken, humble sheds of grace to thee.
Shelter in place of wander, as we see
Up close so long what deserves wondering.
Or will amnesia set in when it's all
Over? What's the over/under on that?
Remember this: we can learn if we fall
In love with falling, the tumble and splat
Of our POV, waking to the gall
Of finding that our mountains are now flat.

5

On finding that our mountains are now flat,
The horizon cracks open like a Jack-
O-Lantern on Devil's Night. It smiles back
Through busted teeth, and we are glad we're at
A new beginning, although we are fat
Still with the old. So what now do we pack
For this journey? There is no settled track
To follow, but there is no standing pat.
Virulent used to be a metaphor.
Now there are no ideas but in things—
Protein-studded virions, their ardor
Hard as facts. Our languages thickening
Sidelong into objects smaller, blunter.
Give us this day our daily misgivings.

6

Give us this day our daily misgivings
As we question what is gift, what is ours,
Who is us. Now that finally the bars
Re-opened, to what will we be raising
Sloshing glasses? If our moist glad-handings
Ever resume, whom will we clasp? Who breathes
And who does not? My Labrador retrieves
What I throw away. I think my fetchings
Will no longer be the same after this.
Or so I hope. But there's no clean slate, no
Way to un-be all that I have been. Kiss
The past good-bye is a nice thought, but show
Me yours and I'll show you mine. What's amiss
Is good, by and by—we take waking slow.

7

Is good by and by? We take waking slow—
Too slow. Then comes the rockslide, a movement
Of what was fixed but needed fixing. Slip
Into the slippery future, moonshot
Of our age, craters and all. A vaccine
Our Apollo, boosters to our wearied
Cells. Then we can take off our masks, packing
Them away for now, our faces nearly
Naked, but for the PPE we can't
Dislodge. Who will we have become, looking
Back, recalling this time of candescence
When skin was made tablet, a new bookfell
Written in penthouse and in tenement
When touch became our common enemy?

Dominion

Normally it doesn't get to me, being
A cashier in a grocery store. I
Am able to get into a groove, or
The groove gets into me, I don't know which.
I think of the sea stories I read when
I was a kid, and sailors sang as they
Pulled up sails or anchors. Of course, I can't
Sing here—it would seem more like some nutty
Musical than the rhythm of bodies
Making work matter. It's everything I
Can do, though, to keep from singing when I
Hear the scanners ping like 80's synth-pop.
My manager would not like that at all.

I was reading the Bible the other
Day. It was Genesis and all the talk
About animals and dominion. I
Started saying out loud "dominion," which
Sounded like a marble in my mouth—smooth
But hard, troublesome, foreign. I know I
Don't feel I have dominion over my
Dog (who does whatever he pleases), let
Alone anything else. Someone may have
Dominion, but it certainly isn't me.

Today I'm listening to the scanners
Go off like crazy because we're busy
Beyond belief, and the scanners sound like
Sonar on World War II ships in movies,
And for a time I imagine that I'm
The sonar guy telling the captain that
We are surrounded by enemy subs.
Then I imagine I am the captain
Telling the panicked sonar guy in my
Calmest voice, "Give them everything we've got,
For, by God, I will have dominion here."

Carole of the Bells

The ringtone on my cell phone
says "Bell Tower" but there's no bell
and the only tower is the cell tower,
a needle in the eye of the sky.

It is like the Big Bad Wolf dressed up
as Grandma, wearing a housecoat
of ulterior motives and half-hearted
disguises. When I was a little girl,

I opened up a rotary phone—
the woodcutter slicing open the Wolf
to reveal an undigested Grandma—
to reveal two bells aching to announce

the next messenger from another world.
I wanted to know such a lovely thing
from the inside out, a concave way
of knowing, a hammered way.

My father often said "Hell's bells,"
and I wondered what those would sound like.
Tearing metal in a car wreck? The scream
before the wreck? The unvoiced regret

of the disguised life before the scream
before the wreck? Or maybe Hell's bells
are the most beautiful bells with the most
stirring sounds never allowed to be rung.

Across the river in Newport, Kentucky
is the World Peace Bell.
It was created for the new millennium.
It weighs 66,000 pounds.

I'm not clear why it's a peace bell.
It isn't rung when peace breaks out.
There's been war somewhere in the world
the entire time since the bell was first rung.

Ringing it doesn't end war.
Seems like a lot of pressure to put on a bell
that just wants to be a bell.
But bells have long carried more than their own weight.

You can put copper and tin together
to get bronze, but if you put war
and bells together, you don't get peace.
There doesn't seem to be an alloy for that.

The hand bell choir at church
is the only place I wear gloves
that are not for keeping out the cold.
They are to keep the oils in, away

from the fragile gleam of the bells,
but they are mostly for show, to say
with our hands rather than our mouths,
this matters more than you know.

I can shake one thing out of this bell.
It's not a magician's hat that spoils
you with a variety that leaves you hungrier
than when you came. I can shake one

thing out of this bell, one pure note
so clear you can bathe in it,
so reliable you can stake your life
on it. Now the sound hides inside,

waiting to be called, waiting to be wanted.
For a thing to do exactly what you ask of it,
lingering after as if to say, "You're welcome,"
"My pleasure," or "Again, again!"

That is a moment not to be taken lightly.
Your asking is not a demand.
You are asking for a thing to be itself,
to do what it does perfectly,

asking nothing less, asking nothing more.
You want what it has to give,
and with such gratitude on both sides,
how can that not be music?

Jupiter

It started small at first, the slightest inconvenience.
Just a little windier than usual, lasting
a little longer. We couldn't eat out on the deck.
A first world problem, I know. Except
it was happening in all the worlds. But kite flying
came back with a vengeance, so it seemed
an even trade. Flag sales took off due to the dramatic
effect, giving nationalism a tail wind.
Then the wind picked up and blew constantly.
All electricity came from wind farms and we powered
everything for free. Lemons kept converting to lemonade.
Until they didn't. The winds grew stronger still until
they tore off the blades of the turbines. Planes could not fly.
Birds tumbled along the ground, their wings a feathery nonsense.
We hunkered down into the local, burrowing.
Cloven into clans, we watch as the soil travels
instead of us. Food is running out. Wind madness—
breakdowns due to the relentless sound and pressure—
is driving us out of our minds and into the vast.
Here there has arisen a cult called Kamikaze
which sees the wind as an angry god ushering in
the Great Cull that will leave a worthy remnant.
I don't expect to be worthy or remain. But I do
think of Jupiter and its Great Red Spot, an anticyclone
as wide as two earths with winds of 400 miles per hour
that has bellowed on for hundreds of years,
without applause or cursing, coursing outside the tiny puff
of human breath, elegant in its ruby distance,
although sometimes beauty up close can
batter us beyond all recognition.

Aubade
> *For Katie*

Someone has re-booted the day
and logged into the sun.
The anti-virus software
is up and running
which keeps out the likes of us
who want the day to go awry.
But I, my love, will find a back door
to restore disorder
so we can lay hold
of what indolence we can find
this morning.
We have locked the bedroom door
against algorithms suggesting
our desires can be bought,
against electronic calendars
which draw and quarter
the river of time.
I am your devoted Luddite
who will protest these incursions
with my whole body.
We won't win in the end.
For now, though, there is only your laugh
caressing my poor joke,
widening the horizon of our bed,
until the patch is in
and we are hauled back
into the applications of stricture.
But know this, my life—
I will ever be your calendar-bane,
your alarm-clock whisperer,
your task-list slayer
as long as the sun
insists on its right
to press *Enter*.

My New Year's Resolutions

I will use lemon Pledge to remove
the waxy build-up of nostalgia.

I will end my affair with Acceleration
and ask Mass for his forgiveness.

I will fake my death and learn what it is
to live without expectations.

I will locate the IP address of my soul
and ping it until I get a response.

I will become a prodigious shirker
of inclement orthodoxies.

I will take lessons in caterwauling
and sing the body entropic.

I will observe the hidden lives of doorknobs,
their gyrations wrangling contiguous worlds.

Minor Loss of Fidelity

I've had Excel on my mind recently,
since I have a lot of time on my hands
these days—not hard time, as they say, but hard
enough for me. Some years back I heard
learning about computers would help me find a job.
I've gotten worse advice, so I did learn
about computers, and I found Excel
to be right up my alley. You see,
I have a head for numbers. Always have.
I don't know what it is. They kinda talk
to me. I know that sounds stupid or crazy,
and it might well be. But that doesn't make it untrue.
Stupid and crazy can be the most irritating
kind of true there is, but there it is.
Excel is a place where there is order,
not in a Nazi kinda way but in the way
your dog knows that if you throw the stick
you won't be gone when he gets back with it.
I'm stunned by how inside that glowing rectangle
waits this formula, so generous, so
open to all. I imagine the cell
as saloon doors, and through them walks the Man
With No Name, tired and bitter and alone,
with fewer friends than he has syllables,
but when he hits the bar, it turns into Cheers,
just without deodorant and with a whole lotta guns.
That's what a good formula can do for you.
It gives a drifting number a place in the cosmos
where things come together.
That gives me hope. But what troubles me
about Excel is versioning. You have this time
capsule, a document in an older version,
and you want to bring it into the light
of the present age in a new version,
but you get this disturbing message:
Minor loss of fidelity. Then it's decision time:

Continue or Cancel? There's a dilemma
we don't often confront, now do we?
I mean, we face it every day, but we don't
confront it. There's another message,
this one *Significant loss of fidelity.*
Sure, that one's a no-brainer. Who would choose
a *significant* loss of fidelity?
Don't need to be Joe College to know you want
no part of that. Have you ever seen
the episode of *Star Trek* (the original one)
called "The Enemy Within"? Of course
you haven't. You have much better things to do
with your time. Let me sum it up for you.
Captain Kirk beams down to the planet
but when he beams back up he is duplicated,
sort of, and one version is the kind,
compassionate but now wimpy Kirk,
and the other version is the bold, decisive
but now nasty zero-inhibitions
Kirk. Now that, my friends, is a significant
loss of fidelity. It's the minor losses, though,
that are trickiest. I mean, how minor's minor?
Do three minor losses make a significant loss?
There are some minor losses of fidelity
we can cancel, if we choose, before they turn
significant. A laugh which leads to a beer
which slides headlong into divorce.
But there are other minor losses where
the *Cancel* button is grayed out and you can only
Continue. Take Alzheimer's, where one day
you forget where you put your car keys,
and heck, who doesn't from time to time,
but it doesn't stop there, until one day
you walk into your favorite bar where everybody
knows your name, except you.

The Sky Sheds a Tear Shaped Like a Black Bird

The sky sheds a tear shaped like a black bird.
This is what happens when one goes away.
The line between falling and flight is blurred.

I know it's your time, your young blood is stirred,
Not shaken, and though the sun shines this day,
The sky sheds a tear shaped like a black bird.

Between you and me such things have occurred,
Good and bad, and there's still more left to say.
The line between falling and flight is blurred.

There is much ahead, you can't be deterred,
But you know how much I wish you could stay.
The sky sheds a tear shaped like a black bird.

Wisdom comes with age, or so I have heard,
But this is a debt that is hard to pay.
The line between falling and flight is blurred.

If only I could give some helpful word
To strengthen you as you enter the fray.
The sky sheds a tear shaped like a black bird.
The line between falling and flight is blurred.

Beginning Acoustics

> *As silence is not silence, but a limit of hearing.*
> Jane Hirshfield, "Everything Has Two Endings"

I want to pick up a piece of granite
from the ground and put it to my ear,
hoping to hear the sea of magma
that orphaned this remnant,
listening for the rising of the batholith
that bore it up, earth's lava lamp
trying to get its groove back.

I want to put my ear to my schnauzer
and hear the howl of the first wolf
who struck a bargain with the bipeds,
to hear if in its voice there was a twinge
of buyer's remorse. Achtung, baby.

I want to sidle up to the fog and listen
to its suspicion of altitude,
its proclivity to cleave.

I want to listen to the oak table
in my dining room and hear the pleasure
of reach shuddering in every limb,
now phantomed, that once coaxed
down the sky from its rectitude.

I want a beetle to belly up to the bar
of my ear's anvil and belt out
the blow-torch song of the exoskeleton,
this Tin Man looking for a heart
in all the wrong places.

I want to hear the Big Bang,
the good vibrations of the Van Allen belt,
the iTunes stored in the Oort Cloud.

But the eye, that overripe fruit,
will have none of it,
for the eye relentlessly smears all
with sight, with its vitreous glare.

Yet when the eyes close
or when the darkness seals us
like an envelope awaiting deliverance,
the unvoiced is voiced
and heralds come to us
from the most unlikely places
with the most unwieldy stories
and all they ask in return
is an audience that remembers
how to be astonished
at what it never saw coming.

Finitude

I

So you're a fish.
It's the thick of the Devonian
the Age of Fish
and life is going—
well, swimmingly
but not for you.
You've been exiled
to the tides and backwaters
trying to avoid
becoming dinner for the despots of the deep
or getting stranded in the mud
by the pesky droughts.
You were made for more,
you think.
So you lift your flat head,
pull yourself up
by your lobed fins,
take a long drag of air,
and check out what's in
the un-sea.

II

So now you're you.
Your fish-self
did all the heavy lifting,
populating the last quarter
of this throbbing planet.
Now you're sheltering
in place
because of COVID-19,

wondering why
the other 18 COVIDs
never broke through
the noise of the day.
What makes 19 special?
Now you're back in the backwater,
in your untidy tidal pool,
devolving.
Or are you?
This circumscription
of your life, this
smalling of the rapacious,
this collapse into finitude
is your evolutionary moment.
You find new uses
for what has been part of you
for eons.
You learn what you don't need
because it's done its job
and it's a new era.
You see how the world outside
changes you
and you change it.
You realize that limits
have their place.
You were made for less,
you think.

morning, morning

In the dream-thin blanket of 4 am
you brought me a thick dictionary
that only defined things the reader is living now
      a lexicon of the present moment
and you pointed with a firm finger
to the entry:
      morning, morning.
The dictionary defined everything
by repeating itself as though
the emphatic was both clarifying
      and mystical
or perhaps it was more like
the way someone shouts
their native language to a foreign speaker
in the hopes that volume
can throw the rock of meaning
through a window
since the door is bolted.
There was something elegant
in the entries' refusal
to let one enter,
in the way insistence
was an invitation anyway.
I searched for
      you, you
and although I looked through
pages and pages
all I found was
      here, here

This Page Intentionally Left Blank

It comes in an envelope,
in a skin luminous
with unfounded expectation,

and with a little force, the envelope
gives up the ghost, gives up the fight,
no longer able to keep the inside in.

Out comes the financial statement,
its dollars and ratios
swirling above the page—

A reckoning
rampant and rampaging,
tiny and trembling.

Then I reach a page still
as a pond, on it only:
This page intentionally left blank.

I can feel the page holding
its breath, counting the seconds,
asphyxiating on Mississippis.

The page reaches for blankness
but cannot leave behind
the smear of intention.

A single set of tracks
in the snow that go all the way
down to the dead ground.

Is this what you intended
when you ended your life
in a fierce declaration of blankness?

I remember the redbird you said
was beating a bitter tattoo
within the drum of your skull.

This was not as it should be.
You so admired how in the world
the redbird's mate was never far away,

how that moving center kept
each bird grounded, even in flight,
as they swirled up beneath

the sun which buffs
the bright and the dun
to a complementary finish.

I was driving home from work tonight
and I-75 filled with brake lights,
making me think of your arteries.

The brake lights were spilling out
the off-ramps and seemed to be
your corpuscles exiting,

each pair trying to find the one
driveway where their engine
could grow cold at its leisure.

Despite your best intentions
blankness evades you still
for I know too much, have kept

your relics in gilt boxes,
secure in the shrine of Our Lady
of the Obstinate Remainder.

Gift

My cat brings me a slaughtered mouse,
his mute gift to one so strange yet so loved.
This is what giving looks like from the inside,
ventricles glowing like a neon storefront sign
crying "OPEN." One sees why humans
have a long history of animal sacrifice.
When words fail or have yet to be invented,
the thrust of gesture gives us courage
to tender what is wounded by our love,
to find a way, however improbable,
to bridge the hollow between giver and receiver.

I broke its neck for you. I flayed its flesh for you.
This could feed me, but I choose to go hungry
and instead eat the pleasure of offering you
something so useless and unwanted in your eyes.
The trail of blood is how I find my way back
to the fierceness of the day, in mourning,
but I will return to this stillness, to you.

Doing and Undoing

The talk of the day passes between
us, water poured across the hands in end-
less repetition, but do we come clean?

The dishes, emails, and other duties
press us like remembered flowers. They bend
our sight away from the fragile beauties

that lurch beneath our notice. Our choices
calcify, leaving fingers that can't rend
the veil. But still, we do have our voices,

don't we? The body heaving up what can't
be held, only heard, somehow always pend-
ing. The voice unfolds, an uncertain slant

of faith, and when votives kindle the tongue,
then the day will not be spoken, but sung.

Nostalgia and Amnesia

> *But yet I know, where'er I go,*
> *That there hath past away a glory from the earth.*
>
> *O joy! that in our embers*
> *Is something that doth live,*
> *That nature yet remembers*
> *What was so fugitive.*
>
> William Wordsworth, "Ode: Intimations of Immortality
> from Recollections of Early Childhood"

The arthropods know this is not
the best of all possible worlds.
The millipedes are nostalgic for
the Carboniferous period when
the air swelled with oxygen
and the furtive could gorge themselves
into extravagance—those halcyon days
when arthropleura was nearly eight feet long,
the largest land invertebrate ever.
Who needed a backbone then
to throw your weight around?

And why so much oxygen?
The trees, formerly such billowy things,
sported their new finery of bark,
and with it, lignin, which stiffened the trees'
resolve. When the trees died, there were not yet
entrepreneurs of decomposition
to take them apart in this theater
of appetites. Incorruptibles,
of sorts, they only succumbed to pressure
as they became time's basement.
The trees hoarded carbon for themselves
until, becoming coal, they would one day
feed the fire that lit our world.

What maple would not long for such a time
before decay's effacing bite?
No doubt the arthropods went around
thanking the trees for their unintended consequences,
for their elegant pageant of causation.

And where did the coal end up?
Folded into mountains
as continents lumbered into one another,
Laurussia smacking into Gondwana
to form Pangea, and with it
the Appalachian mountains.
Once as high as the Rockies,
do the Appalachians long
for a time when they were not
old and hunched, worn down
by erosion's exigencies?
Do they look across this temporary
continent at the haughty Rockies
and mutter under their dusty breath,
Your day's coming?
They know what we do not:
time is not on anyone's side.

In time the Rockies may crumble
Gibraltar may tumble
They're only made of clay
But our love is here to stay.

The faults shake with laughter,
the wind and the rain
cannot contain themselves,
and the oceans roll their many eyes.

The Carboniferous Rainforest Collapse
was a minor extinction event—
unless, of course, you were one
of the extinguished.

With fewer plants, the treasury
of oxygen had been plundered
and poor *arthropleura*
was gasping for its next breath,
which would not come.

This is how a world ends.
Remorseless, implacable.
Things fall into place,
into your place,
and you become a rumor in the night,
half forgotten, half remembered.

Every Road is a Biography

Where, I ask, is the Goober of my dreams,
A hopeful mechanic who sees this life
As a car, knowing it's not as it seems

Because there is a combustible world
Just beneath the polished shine of the hood?
When I was young, the interstates unfurled,

A rippling promise of taming both time
And distance, as well paving a path from
Cities for citizens to flee these prime

Atomic targets. Our hopes and our fears
Congealed like asphalt. Neighborhoods—not mine—
Were erased or maimed. Today no one hears

Their voices, their stories, which are not missed.
When I was young in '59 and we
Passed a Knox Oil station, I would insist

That we'd buy our gas there, so we could get
The "Famous Oklahoma Indians"
Glasses they gave away—eight in a set.

At last my Dad gave in, his will gone weak.
My favorite glass was that of Bacon Rind,
An Osage, standing tall, wearing a sleek

Black otter hat, red shirt, brown wrap, and white
Leggings. Bacon Rind was not his real name,
How could it be? It was not nearly bright

Enough for him called Wah-she-hah, the Star-
Which-Travels. And travel he did, removed
From Kansas to Oklahoma, not far

But stored like unused furniture meant to
Lay forgotten in an untended room. Then
Fortune smiled on the dislodged Osage, who

Later learned of oil beneath their new land.
Wah-she-hah saw to it that they got their
Due, and not a few Osage had their hand

On the wheel of a Pierce Arrow. Where, I
Ask, is the Wah-she-hah of my dreams, who
Stands back, looks out, and says with a slight sigh

As the earth's dark blood pours forth from the lime-
Stone covering its pulsing chambered heart:
"Perhaps things will be different this time."

My One-Sided Conversation with a Stretch of Limestone along I-75

Do you come here often?
How silly of me.
You are not weighed down
by this business of coming and going
as are my kind.

You are defined by *here*.
Or is it that you define *here*?
A bit of both, I suppose.

You still come and go, of course,
but over eons.
Slow motion, fiercer on the slow
than on the motion.
We are all bullied by time.
But you make rest monumental.

Do you miss the waves?
Even from the beginning
you were a boneyard in the making.
You still have a shore, of sorts,
although the traffic of this shore
laps the severed sea.

What was it like before us?
It seems like trying to imagine
who our parents were
before they became parents.
Everything changed with our
charged eyes and marauding hands.

Were you dying
or being born
in the descent
from sea to stone?

A bit of both, I suppose.

So, what I hear you saying is,
I don't have time for this.

Do I have that right?

Come Dew, Come Rust

> *He is that fallen lance that lies as hurled*
> *That lies unlifted now, come dew, come rust,*
> *But still lies pointed as it plowed the dust.*
>   Robert Frost, "A Soldier"

Come, dew,
  lick the broad-faced dawn
like an ecstatic dog.

Come, rust,
  the reddened shoulder-slump
of the declining sun.

Come, dew,
  glaze this earthen vessel,
bring to dirt the glare of art.

Come, rust,
  take our craft and mold it
to your feral purpose.

Come, dew,
  crystal balls of furled futures
anticipating noon's release.

Come, rust,
  let your stigmata bloom
until all is wound.

Come, dew,
  put on your armor of light,
and lead us out of camp.

Come, rust,
  and when we surrender to you,
we will hold nothing back.

Peter Caccavari's poems have been finalists for *Ruminate's* Janet B. McCabe Poetry Prize and *Free State Review*'s Heavenly Creatures Contest. His poems have also appeared in *Connecticut River Review, Dappled Things, The Louisville Review,* and *Cathexis Northwest.* Other poems have been read on Conrad's Corner on WYSO 91.3 FM in Yellow Springs, Ohio and WOSU 89.7 FM in Columbus, Ohio. *Minor Loss of Fidelity* is his first collection of poetry. He has completed a full-length poetry manuscript on mental illness, art, and faith. Caccavari's poetry explores place, form, and character, among other interests. He is Associate Vice President for Institutional Effectiveness at Union Institute & University and a Catholic deacon. He lives in Cincinnati, Ohio with his family.